50 Cakes, Cookies and Confections Recipes

By: Kelly Johnson

Table of Contents

- Chocolate Chip Cookies
- Red Velvet Cake
- Lemon Bars
- Peanut Butter Cookies
- Tiramisu
- Snickerdoodles
- Carrot Cake
- Brownies
- Cheesecake
- Macarons
- Oatmeal Raisin Cookies
- German Chocolate Cake
- Sugar Cookies
- Molten Lava Cake
- Whoopie Pies
- Strawberry Shortcake
- Coconut Macaroons

- Banana Bread
- Funfetti Cake
- Chocolate Truffles
- Icebox Cake
- Biscotti
- Pound Cake
- Rice Krispies Treats
- Linzer Cookies
- Tres Leches Cake
- Florentines
- Angel Food Cake
- Millionaire's Shortbread
- Black Forest Cake
- Madeleines
- Almond Joy Bites
- Coffee Cake
- Thumbprint Cookies
- Pineapple Upside-Down Cake
- Chocolate Fudge

- Baklava
- Apple Crisp
- Magic Cookie Bars
- Churros
- Peanut Brittle
- Cannoli
- Rum Balls
- Marshmallows
- Italian Rainbow Cookies
- Toffee Bark
- Opera Cake
- Snowball Cookies
- Pecan Pie Bars
- Lemon Poppy Seed Cake

Chocolate Chip Cookies

Ingredients:

- 1 cup butter, softened
- 1 cup brown sugar
- 1/2 cup white sugar
- 2 eggs
- 2 tsp vanilla extract
- 2 1/4 cups all-purpose flour
- 1 tsp baking soda
- 1/2 tsp salt
- 2 cups semisweet chocolate chips

Instructions:

1. Preheat oven to 350°F (175°C).
2. Cream butter and sugars until fluffy. Add eggs and vanilla.
3. Mix in flour, baking soda, and salt. Stir in chocolate chips.
4. Drop spoonfuls onto a baking sheet. Bake 10–12 minutes until golden.

Red Velvet Cake

Ingredients:

- 2 1/2 cups flour
- 1 1/2 cups sugar
- 1 tsp baking soda
- 1 tsp cocoa powder
- 1 tsp salt
- 1 1/2 cups vegetable oil
- 1 cup buttermilk
- 2 eggs
- 2 tbsp red food coloring
- 1 tsp vinegar
- 2 tsp vanilla

Instructions:

1. Preheat oven to 350°F (175°C).
2. Mix dry ingredients. In another bowl, mix wet ingredients.
3. Combine both, mix until smooth.
4. Divide into pans and bake 30–35 minutes. Cool and frost with cream cheese frosting.

Lemon Bars

Crust:

- 1 cup butter
- 1/2 cup sugar
- 2 cups flour

Filling:

- 4 eggs
- 1 1/2 cups sugar
- 1/4 cup flour
- 2/3 cup lemon juice

Instructions:

1. Preheat oven to 350°F (175°C).
2. Mix crust ingredients and press into pan. Bake 20 minutes.
3. Whisk filling ingredients, pour over hot crust. Bake 20 more minutes.
4. Cool completely, dust with powdered sugar.

Peanut Butter Cookies

Ingredients:

- 1 cup peanut butter
- 1 cup sugar
- 1 egg
- 1 tsp vanilla

Instructions:

1. Preheat oven to 350°F (175°C).
2. Mix all ingredients until smooth.
3. Roll into balls, flatten with fork in crisscross pattern.
4. Bake 10–12 minutes until edges are golden.

Tiramisu

Ingredients:

- 6 egg yolks
- 3/4 cup sugar
- 1 cup mascarpone cheese
- 1 1/2 cups heavy cream
- 2 cups espresso or strong coffee
- 2 tbsp coffee liqueur (optional)
- 1 pack ladyfingers
- Cocoa powder

Instructions:

1. Whisk yolks and sugar over a double boiler until thick. Cool, then mix with mascarpone.
2. Whip cream and fold in.
3. Dip ladyfingers in coffee and layer with cream mixture.
4. Repeat layers. Chill overnight. Dust with cocoa before serving.

Snickerdoodles

Ingredients:

- 1 cup butter, softened
- 1 1/2 cups sugar
- 2 eggs
- 2 3/4 cups flour
- 2 tsp cream of tartar
- 1 tsp baking soda
- 1/4 tsp salt
- 1/4 cup sugar + 2 tsp cinnamon (for rolling)

Instructions:

1. Preheat oven to 375°F (190°C).
2. Cream butter and sugar, then add eggs.
3. Stir in dry ingredients.
4. Roll into balls, coat in cinnamon sugar. Bake 10–12 minutes.

Carrot Cake

Ingredients:

- 2 cups flour
- 2 tsp baking soda
- 1/2 tsp salt
- 2 tsp cinnamon
- 1 1/2 cups oil
- 1 1/2 cups sugar
- 4 eggs
- 2 cups grated carrots
- 1 cup chopped nuts (optional)

Instructions:

1. Preheat oven to 350°F (175°C).
2. Mix dry ingredients. In another bowl, whisk oil, sugar, and eggs.
3. Combine all and stir in carrots and nuts.
4. Pour into pans and bake 30–35 minutes. Cool and frost.

Brownies

Ingredients:

- 1/2 cup butter
- 1 cup sugar
- 2 eggs
- 1 tsp vanilla
- 1/3 cup cocoa powder
- 1/2 cup flour
- 1/4 tsp salt
- 1/4 tsp baking powder

Instructions:

1. Preheat oven to 350°F (175°C).
2. Melt butter, mix in sugar, eggs, and vanilla.
3. Stir in dry ingredients.
4. Pour into greased pan. Bake 20–25 minutes. Cool before slicing.

Cheesecake

Crust:

- 1 1/2 cups graham cracker crumbs
- 1/4 cup sugar
- 1/2 cup melted butter

Filling:

- 4 (8 oz) cream cheese blocks
- 1 cup sugar
- 4 eggs
- 1 tsp vanilla
- 1 cup sour cream

Instructions:

1. Preheat oven to 325°F (160°C).
2. Mix crust and press into pan.
3. Beat filling ingredients until smooth. Pour over crust.
4. Bake 55–60 minutes. Chill overnight.

Macarons

Ingredients:

- 1 cup almond flour
- 1 3/4 cups powdered sugar
- 3 egg whites
- 1/4 cup sugar
- Gel food coloring
- Buttercream or ganache filling

Instructions:

1. Sift almond flour and powdered sugar.
2. Whip egg whites to soft peaks, add sugar, beat to stiff peaks. Fold in dry mix and color.
3. Pipe onto lined trays. Tap to release air. Let sit 30–60 mins.
4. Bake at 300°F (150°C) for 15 minutes. Cool, fill, and sandwich.

Oatmeal Raisin Cookies

Ingredients:

- 1 cup butter, softened
- 1 cup brown sugar
- 1/2 cup white sugar
- 2 eggs
- 1 tsp vanilla
- 1 1/2 cups flour
- 1 tsp baking soda
- 1 1/2 tsp cinnamon
- 1/2 tsp salt
- 3 cups rolled oats
- 1 cup raisins

Instructions:

1. Preheat oven to 350°F (175°C).
2. Cream butter and sugars. Add eggs and vanilla.
3. Mix in flour, baking soda, cinnamon, and salt.
4. Stir in oats and raisins.
5. Drop onto baking sheet. Bake 10–12 minutes.

German Chocolate Cake

Cake:

- 2 cups flour
- 1 3/4 cups sugar
- 3/4 cup cocoa powder
- 2 tsp baking soda
- 1 tsp baking powder
- 1 tsp salt
- 2 eggs
- 1 cup buttermilk
- 1 cup hot water
- 1/2 cup oil
- 2 tsp vanilla

Frosting:

- 1 cup evaporated milk
- 1 cup sugar
- 3 egg yolks
- 1/2 cup butter
- 1 tsp vanilla

- 1 1/2 cups sweetened coconut
- 1 cup chopped pecans

Instructions:

1. Preheat oven to 350°F (175°C).
2. Mix cake ingredients and pour into pans. Bake 30–35 mins.
3. For frosting: cook milk, sugar, yolks, and butter until thick. Stir in vanilla, coconut, and pecans.
4. Cool cake and spread frosting between layers and on top.

Sugar Cookies

Ingredients:

- 1 cup butter, softened
- 1 cup sugar
- 1 egg
- 1 tsp vanilla
- 2 tsp baking powder
- 3 cups flour

Instructions:

1. Preheat oven to 375°F (190°C).
2. Cream butter and sugar. Add egg and vanilla.
3. Stir in baking powder and flour.
4. Roll dough and cut shapes.
5. Bake 8–10 minutes.

Molten Lava Cake

Ingredients:

- 4 oz semisweet chocolate
- 1/2 cup butter
- 1 cup powdered sugar
- 2 eggs
- 2 egg yolks
- 6 tbsp flour

Instructions:

1. Preheat oven to 425°F (220°C).
2. Melt chocolate and butter. Stir in sugar, then eggs and yolks.
3. Mix in flour. Pour into greased ramekins.
4. Bake 12–14 minutes. Let sit 1 minute, then invert and serve warm.

Whoopie Pies

Cakes:

- 2 cups flour
- 1/2 cup cocoa powder
- 1 tsp baking soda
- 1/2 tsp salt
- 1 cup sugar
- 1/2 cup butter
- 1 egg
- 1 cup buttermilk
- 1 tsp vanilla

Filling:

- 1/2 cup butter
- 1 cup marshmallow fluff
- 1 1/4 cups powdered sugar
- 1 tsp vanilla

Instructions:

1. Preheat oven to 350°F (175°C).

2. Cream butter and sugar, add egg, buttermilk, and vanilla. Mix dry ingredients in and scoop onto baking sheets.

3. Bake 10–12 minutes.

4. Mix filling, spread between two cakes.

Strawberry Shortcake

Biscuits:

- 2 cups flour
- 1/4 cup sugar
- 1 tbsp baking powder
- 1/2 tsp salt
- 1/2 cup cold butter
- 2/3 cup milk

Topping:

- 3 cups sliced strawberries
- 2 tbsp sugar
- Whipped cream

Instructions:

1. Mix strawberries with sugar, let sit.
2. Preheat oven to 425°F (220°C). Mix biscuit ingredients, cut in butter, add milk, and form dough.
3. Cut biscuits, bake 12–15 minutes.
4. Split and layer with strawberries and whipped cream.

Coconut Macaroons

Ingredients:

- 3 cups shredded sweetened coconut
- 4 egg whites
- 3/4 cup sugar
- 1 tsp vanilla
- Pinch of salt

Instructions:

1. Preheat oven to 325°F (160°C).
2. Whisk egg whites, sugar, vanilla, and salt.
3. Stir in coconut.
4. Drop spoonfuls onto baking sheet. Bake 20–25 minutes until golden.

Banana Bread

Ingredients:

- 3 ripe bananas
- 1/3 cup melted butter
- 1/2 cup sugar
- 1 egg
- 1 tsp vanilla
- 1 tsp baking soda
- Pinch of salt
- 1 1/2 cups flour

Instructions:

1. Preheat oven to 350°F (175°C).
2. Mash bananas and mix with butter. Add sugar, egg, and vanilla.
3. Stir in baking soda, salt, and flour.
4. Pour into loaf pan. Bake 50–60 minutes.

Funfetti Cake

Ingredients:

- 2 1/2 cups flour
- 2 1/2 tsp baking powder
- 1/2 tsp salt
- 1 cup butter
- 1 3/4 cups sugar
- 4 eggs
- 1 tbsp vanilla
- 1 cup milk
- 1/2 cup rainbow sprinkles

Instructions:

1. Preheat oven to 350°F (175°C).
2. Cream butter and sugar. Add eggs and vanilla.
3. Mix in dry ingredients alternately with milk. Stir in sprinkles.
4. Pour into pans. Bake 30–35 minutes.

Chocolate Truffles

Ingredients:

- 8 oz semisweet chocolate
- 1/2 cup heavy cream
- 1 tsp vanilla
- Cocoa powder, nuts, or melted chocolate for coating

Instructions:

1. Heat cream until just boiling, pour over chopped chocolate.
2. Stir until smooth. Add vanilla.
3. Chill until firm, then roll into balls.
4. Coat as desired. Chill again before serving.

Icebox Cake

Ingredients:

- 3 cups heavy cream
- 1/2 cup powdered sugar
- 1 tsp vanilla
- 1 box chocolate wafer cookies

Instructions:

1. Whip cream, sugar, and vanilla until stiff peaks form.
2. Spread a layer of whipped cream in a dish, then add a layer of cookies.
3. Repeat layers, finishing with cream on top.
4. Cover and refrigerate overnight until cookies soften.

Biscotti

Ingredients:

- 2 cups flour
- 1 tsp baking powder
- 1/2 tsp salt
- 3/4 cup sugar
- 2 eggs
- 1 tsp vanilla
- 1 cup almonds or chocolate chips (optional)

Instructions:

1. Preheat oven to 350°F (175°C).
2. Mix dry ingredients. In a separate bowl, beat sugar, eggs, and vanilla. Combine all and mix in almonds or chocolate.
3. Shape into a log and bake 25 minutes.
4. Cool slightly, slice, and bake slices 10–15 more minutes until crisp.

Pound Cake

Ingredients:

- 1 cup butter, softened
- 1 1/2 cups sugar
- 4 eggs
- 2 cups flour
- 1 tsp vanilla
- 1/2 tsp salt

Instructions:

1. Preheat oven to 325°F (165°C).
2. Cream butter and sugar. Add eggs one at a time.
3. Mix in flour, salt, and vanilla.
4. Pour into loaf pan and bake 60–70 minutes.

Rice Krispies Treats

Ingredients:

- 3 tbsp butter
- 1 package (10 oz) marshmallows
- 6 cups Rice Krispies cereal

Instructions:

1. Melt butter in a large pot. Stir in marshmallows until melted.
2. Remove from heat and stir in cereal.
3. Press mixture into a greased pan. Let cool before cutting.

Linzer Cookies

Ingredients:

- 1 cup butter
- 2/3 cup sugar
- 2 egg yolks
- 1 tsp vanilla
- 2 cups flour
- 1/2 cup almond flour
- 1/4 tsp salt
- Raspberry jam
- Powdered sugar for dusting

Instructions:

1. Cream butter and sugar, add yolks and vanilla.
2. Mix in dry ingredients. Chill dough.
3. Roll and cut into rounds, with a hole in half for tops.
4. Bake at 350°F (175°C) for 10–12 minutes.
5. Spread jam, sandwich cookies, and dust with powdered sugar.

Tres Leches Cake

Cake:

- 1 cup flour
- 1 1/2 tsp baking powder
- 1/4 tsp salt
- 5 eggs
- 1 cup sugar
- 1/3 cup milk

Milk mixture:

- 1 can evaporated milk
- 1 can sweetened condensed milk
- 1/4 cup heavy cream

Topping:

- 1 1/2 cups whipped cream
- Cinnamon (optional)

Instructions:

1. Bake cake in 9x13 inch pan at 350°F (175°C) for 25–30 mins.
2. Poke holes and pour milk mixture over warm cake.
3. Chill, then top with whipped cream.

Florentines

Ingredients:

- 1/2 cup butter
- 2/3 cup sugar
- 2 tbsp cream
- 2 tbsp honey
- 2 tbsp flour
- 3/4 cup sliced almonds
- 1/4 cup chopped dried fruit or orange zest
- Melted chocolate (optional)

Instructions:

1. Preheat oven to 350°F (175°C).
2. Boil butter, sugar, cream, and honey. Remove and stir in flour, almonds, and fruit.
3. Drop spoonfuls on baking sheet, flatten slightly.
4. Bake 8–10 minutes. Cool and dip in chocolate if desired.

Angel Food Cake

Ingredients:

- 1 cup cake flour
- 1 1/2 cups sugar
- 12 egg whites
- 1 1/2 tsp cream of tartar
- 1/4 tsp salt
- 1 tsp vanilla

Instructions:

1. Preheat oven to 350°F (175°C).
2. Sift flour with 1/2 cup sugar.
3. Beat egg whites with cream of tartar and salt until soft peaks. Gradually add remaining sugar.
4. Fold in flour mixture and vanilla.
5. Pour into ungreased tube pan. Bake 35–40 mins, invert to cool.

Millionaire's Shortbread

Base:

- 1 cup butter
- 1/2 cup sugar
- 2 cups flour
- Pinch of salt

Caramel:

- 1 can sweetened condensed milk
- 1/2 cup butter
- 1/2 cup brown sugar

Topping:

- 8 oz chocolate, melted

Instructions:

1. Preheat oven to 350°F (175°C). Mix base ingredients, press into pan, bake 20 mins.
2. Simmer caramel ingredients until thick and golden. Spread on cooled base.
3. Chill, then top with melted chocolate. Slice when set.

Black Forest Cake

Cake:

- 1 3/4 cups flour
- 3/4 cup cocoa powder
- 1 1/2 tsp baking powder
- 1/2 tsp baking soda
- 1/2 tsp salt
- 1 cup buttermilk
- 1/2 cup oil
- 2 eggs
- 1 1/2 cups sugar
- 1 tsp vanilla

Filling/Topping:

- 2 cups heavy cream
- 1/4 cup powdered sugar
- Cherry pie filling or fresh cherries
- Chocolate shavings

Instructions:

1. Bake cake layers at 350°F (175°C) for 25–30 mins.

2. Whip cream with sugar.

3. Layer with cherries and cream between cakes.

4. Top with cream, cherries, and chocolate shavings.

Madeleines

Ingredients:

- 1 cup all-purpose flour
- 1/2 cup sugar
- 1/2 tsp baking powder
- 1/4 tsp salt
- 2 large eggs
- 1/4 cup melted butter
- 1 tsp vanilla extract
- Zest of 1 lemon

Instructions:

1. Preheat oven to 375°F (190°C).
2. Mix flour, sugar, baking powder, and salt in a bowl.
3. Beat eggs, vanilla, and lemon zest. Fold into dry ingredients.
4. Stir in melted butter.
5. Grease Madeleine pan and spoon batter into molds.
6. Bake for 10-12 minutes until golden. Cool and dust with powdered sugar.

Almond Joy Bites

Ingredients:

- 1 1/2 cups shredded coconut
- 1/4 cup honey
- 1/4 cup almond butter
- 1 tsp vanilla extract
- 24 whole almonds
- 12 oz chocolate (dark or milk)

Instructions:

1. Mix coconut, honey, almond butter, and vanilla in a bowl.
2. Shape mixture into balls and top with an almond.
3. Melt chocolate and dip each ball into it.
4. Set on parchment paper and refrigerate to set.

Coffee Cake

Ingredients:

- 2 cups flour
- 1 1/2 tsp baking powder
- 1/2 tsp baking soda
- 1/2 tsp salt
- 1 cup sugar
- 1/2 cup butter, softened
- 2 eggs
- 1 cup sour cream
- 1 tsp vanilla extract

Topping:

- 1/2 cup brown sugar
- 1/4 cup flour
- 1/4 tsp cinnamon
- 1/4 cup butter, cold

Instructions:

1. Preheat oven to 350°F (175°C).

2. Mix dry ingredients in a bowl. Beat butter, sugar, and eggs, then add sour cream and vanilla.

3. Gradually add dry ingredients. Pour into greased pan.

4. Combine topping ingredients, sprinkle over batter.

5. Bake for 40-45 minutes.

Thumbprint Cookies

Ingredients:

- 1 cup butter, softened
- 1/2 cup sugar
- 2 cups flour
- 1 tsp vanilla extract
- Jam or preserves (your choice)

Instructions:

1. Preheat oven to 350°F (175°C).
2. Cream butter and sugar. Add vanilla and flour.
3. Roll dough into balls and make a thumbprint in each.
4. Fill with jam.
5. Bake for 10-12 minutes.

Pineapple Upside-Down Cake

Ingredients:

- 1/2 cup butter, melted
- 1 cup brown sugar
- 1 can pineapple rings, drained
- 10 maraschino cherries

Cake:

- 1 1/2 cups flour
- 1 tsp baking powder
- 1/2 tsp salt
- 1/2 cup sugar
- 1/2 cup milk
- 1/2 cup butter, softened
- 1 egg

Instructions:

1. Preheat oven to 350°F (175°C).
2. Pour melted butter and brown sugar into pan. Arrange pineapple and cherries.
3. Mix cake ingredients and pour over fruit.
4. Bake for 35-40 minutes. Cool before flipping.

Chocolate Fudge

Ingredients:

- 2 cups semi-sweet chocolate chips
- 1 can sweetened condensed milk
- 1/4 cup butter
- 1 tsp vanilla extract

Instructions:

1. Melt chocolate, condensed milk, and butter in a saucepan.
2. Stir in vanilla.
3. Pour into greased pan and refrigerate for 2-3 hours.
4. Cut into squares and serve.

Baklava

Ingredients:

- 1 package phyllo dough
- 2 cups mixed nuts (walnuts, pistachios, almonds)
- 1 tsp cinnamon
- 1 1/2 cups sugar
- 1 cup water
- 1/2 cup honey
- 1 tsp vanilla extract
- 1 cup butter, melted

Instructions:

1. Preheat oven to 350°F (175°C).
2. Chop nuts and mix with cinnamon.
3. Brush phyllo sheets with butter, layer them, and sprinkle with nut mixture.
4. Cut into squares and bake for 40-45 minutes.
5. Heat sugar, water, and honey until dissolved. Pour over baklava.
6. Let cool before serving.

Apple Crisp

Ingredients:

- 6 cups apples, peeled and sliced
- 1 tbsp lemon juice
- 1 cup oats
- 1/2 cup flour
- 1/2 cup brown sugar
- 1/2 cup butter, softened
- 1 tsp cinnamon

Instructions:

1. Preheat oven to 350°F (175°C).
2. Toss apples with lemon juice and spread in baking dish.
3. Mix oats, flour, brown sugar, butter, and cinnamon to form a crumbly topping.
4. Sprinkle over apples and bake for 40 minutes.

Magic Cookie Bars

Ingredients:

- 1 1/2 cups graham cracker crumbs
- 1/2 cup butter, melted
- 1 can sweetened condensed milk
- 1 cup semi-sweet chocolate chips
- 1 cup shredded coconut
- 1 cup chopped walnuts

Instructions:

1. Preheat oven to 350°F (175°C).
2. Press graham cracker crumbs into greased pan.
3. Layer with chocolate chips, coconut, walnuts, and pour condensed milk over.
4. Bake for 25-30 minutes.

Churros

Ingredients:

- 1 cup water
- 2 tbsp sugar
- 1/2 tsp salt
- 2 tbsp vegetable oil
- 1 cup flour
- 2 eggs
- 1/4 cup sugar (for coating)
- 1 tsp cinnamon

Instructions:

1. Boil water, sugar, salt, and oil. Stir in flour and cook until thick.
2. Let dough cool and mix in eggs.
3. Heat oil for frying and pipe dough into strips. Fry until golden.
4. Mix sugar and cinnamon, and coat churros.

Peanut Brittle

Ingredients:

- 1 1/2 cups sugar
- 1/2 cup corn syrup
- 1/4 cup water
- 2 tbsp butter
- 1 cup peanuts
- 1 tsp baking soda

Instructions:

1. Boil sugar, corn syrup, and water until it reaches 300°F (150°C).
2. Stir in butter and peanuts, cook for 5 minutes.
3. Remove from heat, stir in baking soda.
4. Pour onto greased baking sheet and cool completely. Break into pieces.

Cannoli

Ingredients:

- 1 package cannoli shells
- 2 cups ricotta cheese
- 1 cup mascarpone cheese
- 1/2 cup powdered sugar
- 1/2 tsp vanilla extract
- 1/4 cup mini chocolate chips
- 1/4 cup chopped pistachios (optional)

Instructions:

1. Mix ricotta, mascarpone, powdered sugar, and vanilla in a bowl until smooth.
2. Stir in chocolate chips.
3. Spoon mixture into a piping bag and fill cannoli shells.
4. Optionally, dip the ends in chopped pistachios.
5. Serve immediately or refrigerate.

Rum Balls

Ingredients:

- 1 1/2 cups crushed vanilla wafers
- 1 cup powdered sugar
- 2 tbsp cocoa powder
- 1/4 cup dark rum
- 1/4 cup corn syrup
- 1/4 cup chopped nuts (optional)
- Additional powdered sugar for coating

Instructions:

1. Mix crushed wafers, powdered sugar, cocoa powder, and nuts in a bowl.
2. Add rum and corn syrup, stirring to combine.
3. Roll mixture into small balls and coat with powdered sugar.
4. Refrigerate for at least 1 hour before serving.

Marshmallows

Ingredients:

- 3 packets unflavored gelatin
- 1 cup cold water (divided)
- 2 cups granulated sugar
- 1 cup light corn syrup
- 1/2 tsp vanilla extract
- Powdered sugar for coating

Instructions:

1. Sprinkle gelatin over 1/2 cup cold water and let bloom for 5 minutes.
2. Combine sugar, corn syrup, and remaining water in a saucepan, heating until sugar dissolves.
3. Pour the hot syrup over gelatin and beat until fluffy.
4. Stir in vanilla and pour into greased pan.
5. Let set for 4 hours, then cut and coat with powdered sugar.

Italian Rainbow Cookies

Ingredients:

- 1 1/2 cups almond flour
- 1/2 cup sugar
- 1/4 cup unsalted butter, softened
- 3 eggs
- 1/2 tsp almond extract
- Red and green food coloring
- 1/2 cup apricot preserves
- 8 oz chocolate, melted

Instructions:

1. Preheat oven to 350°F (175°C).
2. Mix almond flour, sugar, butter, eggs, and almond extract.
3. Divide batter into three bowls and color each with food coloring.
4. Layer the colored batters in a greased pan and bake each layer for 10-12 minutes.
5. Spread apricot preserves between the layers and top with melted chocolate. Let cool before cutting.

Toffee Bark

Ingredients:

- 1 1/2 cups butter
- 1 1/2 cups brown sugar
- 1/4 tsp salt
- 2 cups semi-sweet chocolate chips
- 1/2 cup chopped nuts (optional)

Instructions:

1. Preheat oven to 350°F (175°C).
2. Melt butter, brown sugar, and salt in a saucepan over medium heat.
3. Pour mixture over a baking sheet lined with parchment paper.
4. Bake for 10 minutes, then remove and sprinkle chocolate chips over.
5. Spread melted chocolate and sprinkle with chopped nuts.
6. Refrigerate until set, then break into pieces.

Opera Cake

Ingredients:

- 1 batch almond sponge cake
- 1 cup coffee-flavored syrup
- 2 cups chocolate ganache
- 1 cup coffee buttercream

Instructions:

1. Slice almond sponge cake into thin layers.
2. Brush each layer with coffee syrup.
3. Spread coffee buttercream between layers, followed by chocolate ganache.
4. Assemble the layers and refrigerate until set.
5. Garnish with chocolate glaze and serve chilled.

Snowball Cookies

Ingredients:

- 1 cup unsalted butter, softened
- 1/4 cup powdered sugar
- 2 cups all-purpose flour
- 1/4 tsp vanilla extract
- 1 cup chopped nuts (optional)
- Powdered sugar for rolling

Instructions:

1. Preheat oven to 350°F (175°C).
2. Cream butter and powdered sugar. Add vanilla and flour until combined.
3. Fold in nuts (if using).
4. Roll dough into small balls and bake for 12-15 minutes.
5. Roll in powdered sugar while warm.

Pecan Pie Bars

Ingredients:

- 1 1/2 cups flour
- 1/2 cup butter, softened
- 1/4 cup sugar
- 1/4 tsp salt
- 1/2 cup corn syrup
- 1/2 cup brown sugar
- 2 eggs
- 1 1/2 cups pecans

Instructions:

1. Preheat oven to 350°F (175°C).
2. Combine flour, butter, sugar, and salt. Press into a baking pan.
3. Bake for 10 minutes.
4. Mix corn syrup, brown sugar, eggs, and pecans. Pour over crust.
5. Bake for an additional 20-25 minutes.

Lemon Poppy Seed Cake

Ingredients:

- 1 box lemon cake mix
- 1/2 cup sugar
- 3 eggs
- 1/2 cup vegetable oil
- 1/4 cup lemon juice
- 1 tbsp poppy seeds
- 1/2 cup powdered sugar (for glaze)
- 1 tbsp lemon juice (for glaze)

Instructions:

1. Preheat oven to 350°F (175°C).
2. Mix cake mix, sugar, eggs, oil, lemon juice, and poppy seeds.
3. Pour into a greased cake pan and bake for 30-35 minutes.
4. Mix powdered sugar and lemon juice to make a glaze.
5. Drizzle glaze over cooled cake and serve.

www.ingramcontent.com/pod-product-compliance
Lightning Source LLC
LaVergne TN
LVHW061949070526
838199LV00060B/4043